The Passive Way to Passive Income –

A Guide to Turn Key Real Estate Investments

By Whitney Carpenter

The Passive Way to Passive Income

Cover created by: Worx Graphic Design
hello@worxgd.com
Copyright © 2015 By Whitney Carpenter

All rights reserved. This book, or parts thereof, may not be reproduced in any form without permission in writing from the author,
wcarpenter@billwoodproperties.com

The scanning, uploading and distribution of this book via the internet or via any other means without the permission of the author is illegal and punishable by law. Please purchase only authorized electronic editions, and do not participate in or encourage electronic piracy of copyrighted materials. Your support of the author's rights is appreciated. The publisher does not have any control over and does not assume any responsibility for author or third party websites or their content.

Table of Contents

Description 4

Introduction 6

Chapter 1: "Passive Income"
What is it and why is it important? 13

Chapter 2: "The Passive Way"
What is a Turn Key Real Estate
Investment? 22

Chapter 3: "Somebody Said"
The common thoughts of Turn Key Real Estate
Investments.. 32

Chapter 4: "The Properties"
Types of Turn Key Properties 49

Chapter 5: "Property Management" 58

Chapter 6: "Acquisition/Funding" 67

Chapter 7: "The Consensus" 75

Description

So you want to get into real estate? You've worked hard to build your working career and now you're looking for something beyond your retirement plan? Not necessarily looking to build an entirely new trade to get there? You've come to the right place.

In this book, you'll learn that there truly is a HANDS-FREE, yes HANDS-FREE investment strategy in real estate. You'll find that you don't have to be loaded with cash to do so either. Investment in turn key properties is a simple way for the average American citizen to build a sustainable retirement without starting an entire real estate business from the ground up. This means no renovation projects, no landlord nightmares, and no forking over endless amounts of cash because of misguided deadlines and budgets.

Introduction

I've been investing in real estate in some way, shape or form since 2008. Like most investors I've spoken with, my husband and I sort of fell into the industry. UN-like others I've met, we did not have a mentor, a book, a seminar or a Real Estate Investors Association (REIA) to help us get started. We spent the first 5 years of investing giving ourselves a true HANDS-ON investment experience. We acquired properties via home equity line of credit, personal loans, and even refinanced a vehicle to purchase a property. Once we accumulated 10 properties and replaced my income, I started a property management company. This is what changed everything.

Once we opened the doors to Billwood Properties, I started attending networking events to build my business. Through this, I found my local REIA. It was there that I learned about wholesaling, hard money, and plenty of other investment terms that just do not exist in our everyday language. When you think real estate, you most likely think of flipping houses, or being a landlord. It doesn't usually get too much more in depth than that.

When I started learning about these concepts, I soaked every bit of information in like a sponge on a puddle of water. It was so exciting, yet overwhelming all at once. I couldn't figure out where to focus my attention. I was already buying rental properties, I had a growing property management company, I then learned that there were people out there that were willing to loan you the cash to purchase properties AND fund the renovation. Flips were seemingly more and more attractive. My head was spinning!

Through these strategies, I took the most to wholesaling. This may also be known as contract flipping. Wholesaling is the most recommended entry plan into real estate. Mainly because of the low capitol that is perceived to be required to invest. The idea is to negotiate a purchase price of a home and enter into a contract with the seller. The contract can then be assigned to another party for a fee. During my time as a "wholesaler", I was finding great deals, putting them under contract and selling them to other investors for a fee of around $5,000. This was great capitol for me and the strategy was working well until I ran into 2 major issues. These issues just didn't sit right with me. The first occurrence was a property I "sold" to a buyer that did not show up for closing. He just simply changed his mind. I was not in a position to purchase the property myself therefore, the deal fell through. I did not want to be known as the person who puts transactions together and did not have the ability to see them through. I made the decision to continue wholesaling with the condition to only go after a deal that I have the ability to close on personally in the event that the buyer did not come through. Through this decision, I could maintain my reputation while building the capitol I needed with wholesaling.

All was well until the second issue I experienced with wholesaling, I met very inexperienced buyers with cash to purchase. They wanted to build their passive investments through rental properties. GREAT! I sold them a property for $28k that needed roughly $15k in renovations. The property would rent for about $850 per month once complete. The renovation was not too extensive, it was more of a lipstick job. Paint, floors, and kitchen needed a little TLC. Fast forward a few months, the buyers with holes burning in their pockets ended up with a SEVENTY THOUSAND DOLLAR RENOVATION! I could not believe my eyes or ears! Don't get me wrong, this was a beautiful renovation. There was a brand new kitchen with custom cabinets, smooth granite countertops, gorgeous ceramic tile in the kitchen and baths. Talk about top notch! The reality of the scenario is this was a rental property in a rental neighborhood that no matter what you did, it would always rent for $850 per month. I immediately felt guilty for selling them the property. Although I did not oversee their renovation and I educated them well enough to get them on their way, I could not help but feel that I could've done *something* to prevent this from happening. How would they escape this terrible investment? Will they want to continue on investing into real estate? Would they always associate their low or negative cash flow with the deal I sold them? These questions rocked my moral compass to its core and therefore I had to make a change.

My goal was to create an investment opportunity where there was as little guess work as possible with the transaction. I wanted my buyers to experience a product that was cash-flowing with the right kind of renovation for the right amount of income. I wanted the work to be done correctly and to code. I wanted the property to have passed all inspections and be rented legally and with integrity. With this book, I want to teach you how to identify a deal I just described and what to look for in it. You cannot go into any transaction without educating yourself to a degree. This book will help you know what to educate yourself on.

Chapter 1
"Passive Income"

Most of us were brought up on or at least understand the phrase, "time equals money". In my eyes, this could not be any further from the truth. In order to be truly wealthy, you have to find a way to make an income without you physically doing work to obtain it. Your money absolutely cannot depend on your time. There's not a wealthy person out there that will tell you otherwise.

For over 10 years of my life, I worked 40+ hours per week as a waitress at Waffle House. While I am extremely grateful that I am no longer yelling food orders at the top of my lungs in between delivering smothered and covered hashbrowns, I loved my job. My husband, Charlie, was a warehouse laborer and through this, for the most part, we made a good enough living to support our family's modest lifestyle. We lived in our ½ duplex home that we owned free and clear, therefore, our expenses weren't too substantial. All in all, Charlie and I provided ourselves with as much stability as we could, given the "career paths" we had chosen.

There were times, however, that we just could not control. Things got a little tough when I had to take a day off of work for my kids' doctor appointments. I could completely forget about the idea of field trips or anything extracurricular. No matter how much I attempted to make it work, I could not sacrifice the loss of any potential income for work missed. Sure I could easily make up shifts but no matter how many great tips I earned, I could not make a cent if I was not physically there. The option of getting a second job seemed daunting as I'd lose more time with my daughters. There are only so many hours in a work week. Once I had learned that there was no way I could find a genie to grant me a wish of endless time, I realized I needed an alternative to support my family in another way. I needed a passive income.

The idea was to invest into *something* that would bring me some kind of residual income. I researched everything I could on residual income. I had even at one point become a consultant for 2 different multi-level marketing companies. Through those experiences, alongside my extensive research, I quickly realized 2 things. #1 – there are only a few ways to create a passive income and #2 – they all required an investment of some sort to gain that income. What I wanted to explore was the quickest, most reliable source of passive income. There is no avoiding an investment completely. You will have to invest *something* in order to receive the cash flow you are searching for.

The popular paths to passive income that I have found are stocks, businesses and real estate. There are pros and cons to each type of investment and I believe accessibility is going to shape the direction you take.

Although you made the decision to pick up a real estate related book, let's say you have considered investing into the stock market. It would be simple to think one just walks into the office of a stock broker, hands him money, says "make me money" and goes about their day. There are a multitude of things to consider when working with stock brokers. These include investment minimums, trading fees, and commissions. Not to mention, who the heck knows what is really going to happen with your investment. With such rapid changes, it is really hard to tell how well of an investment you will really have made and even keep track of it. While definitely not impossible to make stock investments work, there are more rooted routes to passive income.

Business investments may or may not be more stable than stock market investments. Investing into a business sometimes can take a little time and effort in the beginning in order to get it to the point of passiveness. Depending on the type of business you are investing in, your start-up costs could be substantial. In addition to start-up time and money costs, (unless you are purchasing a franchise) you are going to have to put together a business plan, set up your systems and build a team to get your company to a hands free position. If you choose to invest into a business with a solid plan, it can very well pay off. The question is how much time and money will you have to sacrifice to make it do so?

In choosing real estate as our path to passive income, my husband and I began purchasing properties. The rentals we acquired became our retirement plan. In this, we first calculated what it would cost us to live on a monthly basis. At that time, we figured about $3000 per month. That was about what we made working our 40+ hour work weeks. Sad, but true for us.

Having this number in mind made it very simple to build a plan for a rental portfolio. The average property we could purchase would give us $300 per month cash flow. If we purchased 10 rental properties, the cash flow would replace both of our work weeks. This was the beginning to a whole different mindset than the time equals money concept we were brought up to carry.

With all that I have grown to learn, I wholeheartedly believe passive income is the way to true success and freedom. Choosing the road of passive income through real estate can create a world of opportunity. The reality is creating a solid portfolio in real estate can take time and effort to build. Just as it is with stocks and businesses, there is a lot that goes into a creating a grand slam portfolio. You can spend years educating yourself on the ins and outs of investing into rental properties. Between choosing the type of properties you invest in, the renovation and the rental management, you are looking at a whole other career to build. It does not have to be that way.

There is a way to remove most of the initial sacrifice it takes to become a great real estate investor. You do not have to spend thousands of dollars on training and seminars and hard-knock lessons. This strategy is called turn key investing. Doing this allows you to invest into cash flowing properties without the headache of a renovation or all that comes along with it. Why should you quit your career to become a full time real estate investor? Why should you give up your passion to create a good retirement plan for yourself? The answer is you shouldn't. You deserve to live the life you are currently living while taking the passive way to passive income.

Chapter 2
"The Passive Way"

The idea of "The Passive Way" really means to kick back and enjoy the checks as they come rolling in. In creating this strategy, I found my true passion. I love real estate and everything about it. If you are not in love with the ins and outs of renovations and business management then there is no reason for you to jump in this full time. Your time is valuable and meant to be dedicated to the actions that you are most passionate about. Turn key investments are all about creating an income to cover your expenses to allow you to focus on those passions.

Okay, what is a turn key real estate investment? A turn key real estate investment is the acquisition of a property that is cash flowing the day you purchase. Okay folks, I've answered your question, nothing left to write here. In terms of definition, it really is that simple. My goal here is not to give you a definition repeatedly in the form of drawn out chapters. I want to help give you an understanding of what to expect in a transaction of this sort and make yourself the best passive investor around.

First, let's back up a bit. Let's talk about what a turn key real estate investment is *not*. A TRUE turn key real estate investment does not include any renovations, tenant placement or management of the property on your behalf. It is truly hands-free. Your job as a turn key real estate investor is to sign your name on a deed and collect your profit after expenses every month.

In traditional rental property investments, the first step is to acquire the property. In most cases, to do this with enough room for a positive cash flow, you will need to look for a dirt cheap, ugly house. While there are plenty of strategies out there to obtain these types of houses, let's be real, if you are looking into turn key real estate investment strategies, you probably don't want to market for sellers. You can spend weeks, months, and sometimes even years to negotiate a price that will be appealing for a deal structure you're looking for. This ultimately means you're looking at foreclosed properties. In today's market, there are many bank owned properties available for purchase. Most in the dilapidated shape rehabbers like myself drool over. The problem with these great deals is, no bank is going to finance a property in such poor shape. Before you say, "Well I know a guy who dot dot dot". If you find a bank or mortgage lender who will finance a house with a leaky roof and the copper pipes cut out with reasonable terms, PLEASE give them my phone number. In MOST cases, these transactions are going to require cash to close.

Assuming you have the cash to purchase the property, let's talk about what to do next. You are the proud new owners of 123 Main Street with a free and clear title. YAY! Now all you have to do is figure out how you will fund and manage the renovation. This part of the project requires a large investment of two very important things. Time and money. Neither of which is ideal for a quick, easy, profitable investment.

You may or may not be thinking that the renovation will be the fun part. You have seen plenty of rehab shows and you are pretty handy around the house. Why can't you handle the project on your own? There are quite a few things that take place during a home renovation that real estate TV shows do not necessarily showcase. There are contractors to manage, building codes to comply with, and some areas have lead and rental licensing laws. Not to mention knowing what materials to use to make your rental durable while keeping your project affordable. Remember my good ol' $70k renovation friends? You don't want to end up in their shoes.

To complete a renovation legally, you would need to check with your local code administration to see what sort of requirements there are for building permits as well as rental requirements. In my area, there are requirements to follow in order to ensure your property is eligible for residential rental use. They look at things like smoke detectors in correct locations, GFCI protected electrical outlets within 6 feet of water, and they like to ensure that bedrooms are enough square footage to be considered habitable. These are just some examples of what our local rental code administration looks for. Be sure to check with yours before entering into an investment. It would be terrible to invest and renovate an entire property just to find out that the ceilings wouldn't meet code requirements. Your entire investment would have been a waste.

An ideal renovation can take 90 days or less. During that time, you will have holding costs in addition to the actual renovation. Not to mention the time you will take away from your job and the income lost there. Your holding costs are going to be items such as utility bills, insurance, taxes, and loan payment costs.

Okay, you're a stubborn one. You've bought and renovated the property. Now you've got to do the absolute most important part of your rental investment project. You have to rent it. First you will have to research market rent in your area. Once you decide that, how will you market the property? There are many tools out there that make it simple to market your property online.

If you have your property priced right and decent photos, your phone will be ringing in no time. Which brings me to my next point. Will you have the time to take all of the calls coming in? If you have a full time job, it will be difficult to answer your phone throughout the day.

Once you get to the prospective tenants' phone calls, you will need to show them the property. With your busy work schedule, you will most likely have to do showings in your personal time. This is the exact opposite of passive. Not to mention you still haven't even rented the place yet. Meanwhile, those holding costs have not disappeared.

Now that you have shown the place and narrowed down your prospective tenants list, you have got to choose the best candidate. Screening is the absolute most important part of choosing a tenant. You want to be sure you are well equipped with the tools to do so. You will need to run a credit check, criminal check, verify their landlord reference and income. Finding the resources and educating yourself on what to look for can be time consuming. This is not what you should aspire to experience in your quick, hands free investment.

Are you prepared to become a full-time landlord? This is usually the scariest part of the investment. The idea of turn key real estate investments is not to build a team of contractors, realtors, and property managers, and spend the next few years teaching yourself the ins and outs of rental properties. The purpose is to save yourself time and money with a hassle free transaction. You are looking for a passive way to create a passive income. Real estate is an intoxicating industry. It is very easy to jump in completely and hope for the best. With a turn key real estate investment, you're taking a ton of guesswork out of the equation. The acquisition includes the renovation, therefore, you are not estimating those costs. The rent is already set in place, so you know exactly what your return will be. This is about as passive as it gets in real estate.

Chapter 3
"Somebody Said"

The absolute most common response you will have when mentioning turn key investments is, "You will have no control of your own investment". It's in the majority of articles I've read about the subject. What does it really mean? What won't you have control over? Let's see, what types of issues would one say about the control of a rental investment?

The property- "You don't know what you are buying".

I don't know about you, but I am not usually a site unseen sort of investor. If I am going to purchase a property, I would like to see, smell and touch the place so I know what sort of issues I may encounter. Why would that differ with a turn key investment? If you are purchasing a property from a self-proclaimed turn key company and they will not allow you to walk through the property before you agree to purchase, come to a screeching halt. I mean skid your tires and make smoke rise because you DO NOT want to work with this company. This is a serious red flag. A company that offers turn key investments as part of their products and services will not only want you to see the property, they will be overjoyed to do so. As mentioned in the previous chapter, a true turn key real estate investment includes management of the property. The company you work with is not going to want to create more work for themselves. They are going to do all that they can to reduce unforeseen issues to ensure that their job is a walk in the park.

When purchasing a turn key property, use your better judgement. Do a walkthrough of the property and ask if it was renovated with permits. In most cases you will find that the answer is yes. The company has every incentive to do so because it is their name on the line. You can also request a home inspection. This can be very beneficial because the inspector can give you an idea of a timeline for some of your major components of the home. He/she can tell you how long it will be until you have to replace the roof, furnace, water heater and other potential expenses of that nature. This is extremely helpful in estimating long term costs of the property as well as identifying any shoddy work done during the renovation.

On the next page you will find a basic checklist of things to check out when walking through a property. It may be helpful to hire a contractor to walk through the property with you. They may be able to help you identify the condition of some items to look over in the home.

Walkthrough Checklist

GROUNDS

Condition (include deck, driveway, landscaping, fence, etc.)?

EXTERIOR
Foundation need repair? YES   NO
Roof Condition :

Gutter Condition?

Exterior Type?

Condition?

Garage? Condition?

INTERIOR
Windows & Doors:

Flooring:

Kitchen:

Bathrooms

Slab   Crawl Space   Basement   Finished? _____
Basement dry? _____   Sump Pump? _____
Painting

Interior:

Drywall:

SYSTEMS

Electric Condition? _____

　　Water Heater

SEPTIC TANK   SEWER   CITY WATER   WELL   SPRING

APPLIANCES
　Appliances included:

Price – "You're going to overpay for the property".

First, I'll say, you will be paying what I call a convenience fee to the company selling you the property. There is no doubt about it. If that company were not making any money off of the properties they are selling then you would have to wonder why they are offering the product in the first place. It's just the cost of doing business.

When purchasing a turn key real estate investment, or any investment for that matter, it's up to you to decide how much return you are willing to make. No one can tell you that you have overpaid for a property if it is bringing exactly what you expected. If the property is cash flowing what you were hoping, then who cares what the next guy is making as long as your slice of the pie is enough to fill you up.

Some ways you can determine the property value is to get a real estate agent to compare to similar properties in the area or even order an appraisal. Doing so will help you determine the retail value of the property rather than the cash flow potential.

When looking at comparable properties in the area, you want to find as many similarities as you possibly can. Look at the number of bedrooms, number of bathrooms, square footage, property type (single family, ½ duplex, cape-cod, townhouse, colonial, etc.), age of the home and even the features of the property. I try to narrow my search to 3 of the most similar properties in close proximity that have sold within the past 6 months. Once I have those properties, I take the average of the 3 to come up with the Fair Market Value (FMV). I then compare the FMV to the potential purchase price of the property I am interested in. The other thing to look at is the comparable rent in the area. Ask a local property manager or real estate agent to let you know what the going rent rates are for a property similar to your potential investment. You can use this worksheet to help identify a fair purchase price for your turn key investment.

Market Value Worksheet

Address	# of BR & BA	Sq Ft & Lot Size	List Price	Year Built	DOM (Days on Market)

Date Last Sold: _____

Last Sold Price: _____

Market Value Analysis

Find 3-5 Most Comparable Sold Properties, Calculate the Average

Address	# of BR & BA	Sq Ft & Lot Size	List Price	Year Built	DOM (Days on Market)

Management- "You have no idea what kind of tenant you'll be stuck with"

This statement is true. It doesn't matter how you acquire a property, this statement will be true. You can, however, take steps to ensure you aren't putting yourself in a predicament.

    1) Do the walkthrough we talked about before. A lot can be told by looking at a person's living space.

    2) Interview the company's property manager. Get to know the person who may be in charge of the property you are looking to obtain.

    3) Ask for the records. This will give you an idea of how well the property is actually

performing as well as an indication of how well the property manager keeps activities documented.

4) If possible, meet the tenant.

Some records you may want to request should include the rent roll of the property, any leases (including end dates), any history of inspections or citations on record, previous maintenance requests, an income statement and the estimated recurring costs.

The rent roll will tell you the current status of the rent on the property. Most will include the market rent and the current rent. You will see the current vacancy rate and any outstanding balances owed. This can be very helpful to know whether or not the rent is worth counting on in your turn key real estate investment.

Rent Roll

Address	Tenant	Market Rent	Rec. Charge	Lease Start	Lease End	Dep. Held	Bal. Due
123 Main St	Sara Smith	850	850	1/1/2015	1/1/2016	850	400
456 South St	John Johnson	575	450	1/15/2007	MTM	450	0
789 North Ave	VACANT	750	0	VACANT	VACANT	0	0
Total Portfolio		2175	1300	67.7% OCC.		1300	400

Most times when purchasing a turn key investment property, you are subjecting yourself to the terms of the lease that the company has set. You should take time to review the terms you will assume. Some key things to look for in the lease are the start and end dates, rent amount, any utilities included, security deposits held, and total occupants listed. There are many other things you may want to review and the preference on some of those things will vary from buyer to buyer. This can be the preference of pet and smoking policies, appliances provided by owner and maintenance responsibilities.

When you review the history of inspections, not only are you reviewing any problems noted by an authority, you will know how the manager has addressed the issues. This can be telling in how well the property has been maintained. This idea applies when reviewing maintenance requests as well.

The income statement on the property is a little different than the rent roll. The income statement is a summary of the net income on the property. This should include the recurring as well as one-time expenses.

Taking these few actions can help save you a ton of headaches. When purchasing a turn key property you have to use your better judgement. Make sure you are doing research on the property as well as the company to make your investment as sound as possible. There is no way to evade problems all together with a business, but it is possible to make things as simple and hassle free as possible.

Ownership –

This one is actually not mentioned nearly as often as I thought it would be. One thing you need to consider with purchasing a turn key real estate investment property is the ownership you actually have in the property. Often times, investment properties are bought and sold under Limited Liability Companies or "LLC's". Sometimes, for one reason or another, the transaction results in your purchase of the LLC and not the actual property. When a property is purchased using an LLC, the LLC owns the company and the person representing that LLC is called a "member". In some cases, to simplify the deal the LLC membership is sold. This allows the new member to control the LLC's assets which will most likely be the property in question.

While purchasing a turn key investment property this way, make sure there is documentation filed with your state stating that you represent 100% of the LLC.

You do not want to unwillingly go into a deal with any other members on the LLC.

The simple solution for this is to verify or ask your settlement attorney to verify and document this information for you.

In all of the beware notions we have gone over, you can easily see that you have the ability to see your transaction to success. Take a few steps to understand your investment and get to know the experts! Ask questions, do research, and make yourself an educated passive investor.

Turn Key Real Estate Investment Questions

1) Does this acquisition include property management? May I schedule a meeting with the property manager?

2) What repairs were made to the property and what maintenance issues should I expect to incur within the next 2 years?

3) What is the financial history on the property? (Maintenance expenses, actual collected rent, rent payment history, etc.)

4) How is the property deeded? Do you own the property? Will there be an LLC transfer?

Chapter 4
"The Properties"

Now that we know what a turn key property investment is and all of the benefits of purchasing one, let's talk about the properties you are purchasing. The success of a turn key acquisition or any property acquisition for that matter is defined by the cash flow. It does not matter if the property cost $30,000 or $300,000, as long as it cash flows you are in the clear. The lower priced properties almost always seem more attractive than spending more. If the cash flow is the same on a lower priced and higher priced property, one would think it is more beneficial to purchase lower.

In my market, the average rent for a 3 bedroom house in city limits is $850 per month. The cost of a property of this sort as a turn key real estate investment will be around $50,000. This is the type of turn key property I specialize in.

The first client I sold a turn key property to was Matt Garner. Matt is an avid investor. He holds a rental portfolio of an estimated 50 units. When it came to buying the turn key property I had available to him, it was a no brainer. He used all of the tools he had to evaluate any other rental property and just applied it to this one. This particular property was a 3 bedroom 1 bathroom single family home. It was situated on a quiet street within city limits. The home had beautiful wide plank hardwood floors that we stained with a dark cherry finish. Ah! Talk about gorgeous! There was a separate living room and dining room and a fairly decent sized kitchen. We went with white cabinets and a brown/tan speckled laminate counter top. All of the walls in the house were painted tan, Mesa Tumbleweed is the name of the color if that's vital information. With the tasteful contractor grade renovation, we were able to rent this house for $900 per month.

Matt purchased the property for $46,000 with cash. Through his other investments, he was in a position to do so. The recurring expenses on this property are taxes and insurance. The taxes were roughly $1200 annually and insurance around $800 per year. The tenant was responsible for all utilities.

Factoring the expenses and the rent, Matt will pay this property off within 7 years. Think about that cash flow he will have for his retirement years!

Matt's Investment Breakdown

Invested - $46,000 CASH

Annual Income - $10,800 (Rent X 12 months)

Recurring Expenses - $2,000   (Taxes and Insurance)

Vacancy/Misc. - $ 1,800

Net Annual Income - $7,000

$46,000 (Initial Investment) divided by $7000 (Net Income) = 6.57 years to pay off this property.

During my research of turn key companies in the country, properties of this description seem to be the most commonly priced property available. It's affordable to obtain, pays itself off quickly and is a great benefit as a long term investment. Often times though, there is not much equity left in these low end properties. If you are investing for true long term, passive income, this should not concern you. In this case, cash flow is king.

There are, however, benefits to purchasing properties that cost a little more as well. First, there is the equity we just mentioned. There are other reasons someone might want to invest in these property types as well.

Let me tell you about my friend Drew Parker. Drew is fairly new in the rental investment world. He is very active in his research of real estate and asked several great questions when it came to purchasing a turn key property. He had equity in his personal home and was able to do cash out refinance to obtain the funds to purchase some investment properties. With the funds in hand, Drew decided he was interested in a 2 bedroom 1 bathroom ½ duplex that we were selling for $36,500. This home was on the smaller side but the rent was $795 per month making its potential cash flow an estimated $300 per month. With this being Drew's first investment in real estate, he ensured he took all of the steps necessary to cover his bases. He ordered a home inspection and there were some items that arose. Some of the issues were a chimney that needed repointed and some spouting repairs we had not noticed. As an active investor these items were not a large concern for me. They were however a little worrisome for Drew. His concern drifted towards other items that may have issues in the future. The fact that there were any notes from the inspector made Drew realize that he would rather spend more to have to deal with less later on. This meant purchasing a property built more recently with less maintenance over the course of 20 plus years.

This was a great experience for both Drew and I. He walked away from that deal and as perplexed as I was in the beginning, I quickly realized that everyone's bottom line is different. Shortly after, I ran into Drew and he mentioned that he purchased 2 townhomes in a suburb for around $100,000 for each one. The rent was estimated to be roughly $1250 - $1350 per month making the cash flow about the same as the $36k property. The difference for him was the newer property passed the home inspection with flying colors and he would not have any estimated maintenance issues arise any time soon.

I was happy to hear Drew knew what he was comfortable with and went with it. It's extremely important to know where you fit in the investment industry. Just as I was no longer okay with wholesaling properties, Drew was not okay with trading a low upfront investment with the possibility of long term maintenance.

Make sure you think about what type of property you are looking to purchase as your turn key investment. Research the company you may be looking to purchase from to ensure their product and services match up with your needs.

Chapter 5
"Property Management"

Management of your turn key property is vital to the success of your investment. Before contracting to acquire the property, schedule an interview with the property manager. You want to ensure that this person will be a good fit for you. In my experience, there are many great property managers out there that may not necessarily be the best solution for you. A few things you should look for in a property manager are their tenant screening process, their communication process and the maintenance protocol among other things.

The tenant screening process is extremely important because this is the person who is going to make or break your investment success. You want to do all that you can to reduce any risks you can incur. You're going to want your property manager to check the tenant's credit and criminal history, the employment and income verification, and the landlord check. Now, there may be varied stances on the landlord reference. As a property manager, I've found that often times a current landlord will give you false information on a tenant for the sake of relieving their problems. With that, I do not rely on landlord reference as heavily as I do other sources of tenant screening.

When it comes to an applicant credit check, I am not extremely picky with their score or even items on the reports. Why? Of course we'd all love to have a tenant with an 800 credit score and a great paying job.

The reality is if this person possesses these qualities, chances are they would be purchasing a home and not renting. What I look for specifically on a credit report is any utility bills in collections or landlord issues. What I also look for is any history of the same type of collection. For example, if the applicant has 3 very high collections from different cell phone companies, that's a red flag. If they are willing to switch from company to company while never satisfying their previous debt, chances are they will do the same with your rental property.

Looking at credit history in this way can help you gain an idea of prospective tenant's habits without giving you unrealistic expectations. An applicant may have medical bills and maybe even credit cards in default. My optimism tells me that they have chosen to allow their housing costs maintain their priority. This gives you a good chance of receiving your rent even if there is a financial strain for them.

The employment and income verification is the holy grail of the tenant screening process. No matter how nice, clean, and non-criminal a person is, if they do not make enough STABLE income, it will not work out. You'll want to verify the records of the income verification with your property manager. My company requires that the tenant makes a total gross income of a least three times the monthly rent. Ask the property manager what their requirements are.

In addition to good screening practices, your property manager should have a strong communication system for their clients. A day in the life of a property manager can be extremely hectic and very unscheduled. Your property manager should have a means of communication through all of the tasks they manage throughout the day. This can be in the form of a monthly statement with status updates on your units. You should expect a phone call for emergencies. Ideally, (if you're a modern day person), you would like a property manager with an online software you can access 24/7. They can update the software regularly and you can have information on your properties. Through this method you can eliminate the need to speak with the manager directly. This allows the manager the time and freedom to effectively manage your units. This can be good to know if/when there are any maintenance issues as well as what was done to resolve them. Your property manager does not have to have state of the art software. You just need to have the confidence that you can know what is happening with your properties without having to micromanage your manager.

In addition to reporting protocol, you will want to know the property managers maintenance process. In my company, we have a maintenance manager. All of our maintenance calls are routed directly to him. He manages a team of 5 and will decide the priority level of the call then respond accordingly. Maintenance and repairs are inevitable with property ownership. You want to be sure you can trust the person handling them.

Some things to expect on a typical monthly statement would be any funds collected on your behalf. You should see details of the dates the income was collected as well the amount. Next you should see any deductions. Deductions would include fees to the management company, funds held for maintenance reserve, and any expenses paid on your behalf. After that you will see your net profit. This is your magic number. This will tell you how well or poorly your property is doing. There are endless versions or varieties of property statements but the key information is the same. It will include the gross collected rent and the expenses for the month.

On the next page you will find a sample monthly rental property statement.

Sample Monthly Statement

Income			
Date	Income Category	Amount	Description
01/01/14	Rent	$2100,00	January Rent
Total Income		$2100.00	

Expenses			
Date	Expense Category	Amount	Description
01/01/14	Management Fee	$210.00	Monthly Management Fee
01/30/14	Repairs	$52.82	Replace Kitchen Faucet
01/30/14	Cleaning and Maintenance	$7.14	Home Depot

Taking the time to ensure your property manager has these items covered can save you countless headaches and money in the long run. While your goal is to be hands free, you want to validate your investment with a strong management team.

Chapter 6
"Acquisition/Funding"

Funding and acquiring a turn key property can be a never-ending discussion. There are many ways to acquire a property. There's cash, of course, bank financing via residential loan, bank financing via commercial loan, lines of credit, personal loan, even credit cards. There are many other means of funding available. We are going to go over the most common.

Cash is the simplest, most efficient way to do any sort of business. You've heard the saying, cash is king. When acquiring a turn key property using cash, you are buying yourself a quick, seamless transaction. Your negotiation remains between you, the seller and your settlement attorney or agent. This option sometimes can give you a little negotiation power as well. Although most turn key companies have calculated their prices carefully and there may not be much negotiation room, it cannot hurt to try, especially with cash.

When purchasing this way, the seller hears, "simple, quick closing". This can drive the deal in your favor. In most cases, the seller of a turn key investment property is looking to have a very straightforward deal.

Financing and other transaction types may add to closing timelines. The lender may require additional repairs or documents. While the seller is not likely to be shaken by those things, if there are multiple offers the quickest, easiest one may be more enticing.

If you are limited on cash and decide to go all in on a property, you may not necessarily be making a poor decision. Once you make that cash investment you now have yourself a debt-free investment with equity that any bank will proudly loan you money on. This can be helpful in growing your portfolio.

Once you purchase a property with cash, you can do what is called a cash out refinance and purchase another property as cash and continue that cycle to maximize your growth. This is actually how I started my rental portfolio. My husband and I purchased our first house for $25,500 cash. When we were looking to get our rental, we used the equity in the first home to purchase the next.

The equity loan we used was a residential bank loan. The programs vary in terms and requirements. The point I want to note is through a residential loan for investment, you are still personally guaranteeing that loan. There are limits on how many you can do this way, again, that varies by the bank and the programs offered.

Residential mortgages can be beneficial in turn key transactions even without purchasing the home as cash first. If you are looking to acquire the property initially with a residential loan, you can do this sometimes with little down payment. Check with your local mortgage lender or bank loan officer to learn the terms that are available to you.

Jason Baxter recently purchased a turn key investment property from me using a residential mortgage. The purchase price was $45,500 on a property that rents for $850 per month. The lender Jason used required a 20% down payment on his loan. The reason for this requirement was because the use of the property was for investment purposes. The mortgage on the property is approximately $400 per month. The positive cash flow on this property is $450 per month! With an investment less than $10,000, this was a great choice for Jason.

A commercial loan for turn key investment properties is very similar to that of a residential loan. Your scenario is going to be very similar to Jason's. There are some cons to a commercial loan. One downfall could be a demand feature on the loan. Which in a nutshell means the bank can require you to pay your debt in its entirety if they deem necessary. There is also the possibility of adjustable interest rates. The pros to a commercial mortgage are the flexibility, creative loan types and sometimes ease of qualifying. Most of the time, the qualification requirements can depend on the actual asset and not just your personal income. Of course the bank is going to want to see your personal income but factoring in the properties ability to cash flow is a large bonus.

One creative loan type would be a line of credit. The huge benefit to this is to have the ability to purchase as cash (remember quick, seamless) then refinance to another loan type, possibly saving the cost of a down payment.

When obtaining a loan for real estate investments, check with your lender to see what terms you are agreeing to so you can make a sound decision on the best option for you.

An interesting way to purchase your turn key investment is to convert your 401K into a self-directed IRA. In doing so, your IRA can purchase a property and allow the profit to return to your retirement account. As a long term investor, this can be extremely beneficial. There are no restrictions on where or what type of real estate investment you can purchase. One requirement is that all profit returns back to the retirement account. This strategy is extremely beneficial if you do not have access to enough cash to purchase.

It would be wise to speak to your local retirement account expert to know details and terms available to you. That person or company would be able to guide you on your path to building your passive income.

There are many possibilities of acquiring a property. The existence of turn key real estate transaction means there's no reason for you to be undeserving of your passion, career AND strong wealth plan.

Chapter 7
"The Consensus"

The meaning of being wealthy is to have your passive income exceed your personal expenses. Deciding how to build your passive income is no easy feat. Taking years to understand and build a business plan does not seem ideal if your passion lies in another field. Turn key investment properties allow anyone the opportunity to build their wealth easily.

Taking a few steps to understand how turn key investments work can help make your transactions seamless as well as avoid major issues later. Understanding the benefits of this strategy limits opportunities for you to be taken advantage of.

The idea of turn key investments is not to build a team of contractors, realtors, and property managers, and spend the next few years teaching yourself the ins and outs of rental properties. The purpose is to save yourself time and money with a hassle free transaction.

It is my hope that you've walk away from this book with a good understanding of how turn key investments work and feel confident about your purchase. Sit back, relax and enjoy your journey to wealth. You deserve it!

About The Author:
Whitney Carpenter

Whitney Carpenter is a professional business woman, entrepreneur, mother and author. Her dream of owning her own business came when she opened her company Billwood Properties. She had grown tired of punching the clock for someone else and working tirelessly. She had envisioned a better, happier life and she went for that! Her property management company and property investments have allowed her to build a comfortable and lucrative lifestyle. Whitney has chosen to share her expertise in the real estate field in hopes to assist those looking for a change to take the chance and build a lifestyle that they have always dreamed of. You can reach Whitney at www.billwoodproperties.com.

Testimonials

Rochelle Mazza reviewed **Billwood Properties** — 5★

September 16 at 9:41am

These ladies are the best ... must give them much respect they made things possible for me in a time I desperately needed it . So THANK YOU !!! May your continued success be blessed .

Laura Wallace
You made my day! It's so amazing to work side by side with fire starting entrepreneurs like you. You're creating a path like no other, one that lifts those around you while you pursue your dreams. You're doing amazing things and the Worx gals are happy to a part of it!

Cathy Smith ▶ Billwood Properties

27 mins · Hagerstown, MD

I can honestly say that I have watched this company being built from the ground up. Seeing the owners and employees learn and grow as they encouraged each other and our community daily has truly been inspirational to me. I don't know too many other businesses that has the compassion for their communities nowadays. Continue to grow strong and be a Pilar in this community!

The Passive Way to Passive Income

Whitney Carpenter

www.ingramcontent.com/pod-product-compliance
Lightning Source LLC
Chambersburg PA
CBHW060411190526
45169CB00002B/847